Elena

Diane Stanley

HAMPTON-BROWN

THE EXCHANGE

**How much
should people sacrifice
for their families?**

Hampton-Brown
P.O. Box 223220
Carmel, California 93922
800-333-3510
www.hampton-brown.com

Printed in the United States of America

ISBN-13: 978-0-7362-2778-0
ISBN-10: 0-7362-2778-4

07 08 09 10 11 12 13 14 10 9 8 7 6 5 4

FOR THE CHILDREN OF HOUSTON
ELEMENTARY-INTERMEDIATE SCHOOL,
EL PASO, TEXAS, WHO ASKED ME TO WRITE
SOMETHING FOR THEM

* * * * * *

AND ESPECIALLY FOR THE REAL ELENA

Author's Note

My grandmother loved to travel, and she loved to tell stories. Many years ago, on a trip to Mexico, she met a woman named Elena. They liked one another right away, and they became lifelong friends. Elena and my grandmother traveled all over Mexico together.

One afternoon in 1955, Elena and my grandmother were having lunch in a hotel dining room in Monterrey. Elena began to tell the story of her family, and my grandmother **listened in rapt silence, enthralled**. She never forgot it.

Over the years, I often heard my grandmother tell Elena's story, and before she died, she included it in a manuscript of her childhood memories.

Almost fifteen years later, I found it. Then I called Elena, by then in her eighties, and asked if I could write her family story in a book for children. She gave her permission, and once again, she told it—this time to me. So what you will read in this book is true, even the parts you might not believe.

In telling it, I have done three things. First, I have simplified—**and occasionally altered**—some of the scenes to make the narrative flow more naturally. Second, I **put myself in the minds of** Elena and Rosa, adding details out of my imagination. And lastly, I changed some names. All these years I have thought of this as Elena's story, yet when I sat down to write it, I realized

....

listened in rapt silence, enthralled listened to every word with joy and delight

and occasionally altered and sometimes changed

put myself in the minds of tried to think like

that it was really the story of her mother, María. Because I really wanted Elena's name on the book, I altered the names in the story, calling the mother Elena and the daughter Rosa.

When the real Elena grew up, she returned to Mexico, where for a while she taught English. Later she opened a store in Monterrey, where she sold art and antiques. She married and had two children, a boy and a girl. They both live in Texas. Her son, Pepe Luis, is an artist, **a sculptor in wood**. The girl, Susana, speaks four languages and works as a tour guide for **international visitors**. She is married to an astronaut. Elena has two homes, one in Texas and one in Guadalajara, Mexico, not far from the little village her family left so many years ago.

....

a sculptor in wood a person who makes art from wood
international visitors tourists

BEFORE YOU MOVE ON...

1. **Author's Purpose** Why did the author write this story?

2. **Viewing** Look at the map on page 4. What is the name of the town where Elena lived?

LOOK AHEAD Read pages 7–10 to find out about Elena's family.

Rosa tells the story of her mother, Elena. Elena lives in a lovely town in Mexico. She wants to study books and marry Pablo. Her father does not agree.

Chapter 1

My grandfather wanted sons. Instead, God gave him Susana, Anita, María, Margarita, and Elena. In his big cool house in the mountains of Jalisco, Mexico, his five daughters bloomed like flowers in a quiet garden.

In the mornings they sat together on the *veranda* and **embroidered white linen with little birds and curling vines**. As they sewed, they gossiped and laughed. They told stories about the boys they knew and wondered which of them might make good husbands.

In the afternoons, when they awoke from

....

embroidered white linen with little birds and curling vines sewed little birds and curling vines on white cloth

their *siestas*, they sat in the shady parlor and drank lemonade while their father read the newspaper or worked on his **accounts** at a big oak desk.

Every Tuesday, Señor Vargas would come and give them dancing lessons. On the other days, Susana would play the guitar while her four sisters **joined their sweet voices to** the soft music. They would sing traditional songs and love songs. But most of all they **gave their hearts to** the sad songs because those were the most romantic and none of the girls had ever **known any real sorrow**.

Of course, they also helped their mother around the house. There were flowers to be arranged in vases, dresses and shirts and trousers to be made, buttons to be sewn back on. Every meal had to be planned and prepared. The table must be set properly with a clean cloth, and the forks, knives, and spoons

....

accounts money records
joined their sweet voices to sang along with
gave their hearts to loved to sing
known any real sorrow suffered very much in their lives

must be in their correct places. All these things had to be done so their house would remain the lovely and peaceful place it was. It was important that the girls learn these **womanly arts**, for someday they would have husbands and houses of their own. Then they would teach these things to their daughters and **the circle would be complete**.

My mother, Elena, was the youngest. She was different from her sisters. There was a restless spirit in her, a strong imagination. She wanted to do more than sing and sew and cook and dance. She longed to visit distant places and learn other languages. She wanted to read books, as her father did, and **master the magic of numbers**. And sometimes, when she was with her sisters and they were talking or singing, **her mind would drift away into** that other world that was open to boys

....

womanly arts special jobs for women

the circle would be complete the knowledge would go from one generation to the next, like a circle

master the magic of numbers learn mathematics

her mind would drift away into she would think about

but not to her. At first, she tried **to put these thoughts out of her mind** and accept the role that she had been given. But the longing did not go away. It bothered her like a buzzing fly, always **hovering about** and coming right back whenever she brushed it away.

....

to put these thoughts out of her mind not to think about these things

hovering about staying close

BEFORE YOU MOVE ON...

1. **Comparisons** Elena had four sisters. Reread page 9. How was Elena like her sisters? How was she different?

2. **Setting** Describe Elena's home in Jalisco, Mexico. Tell what she and her sisters did there.

LOOK AHEAD Read pages 11–13 to find out what Elena and her parents disagree about.

At last Elena went to the priest of the village. He was the one who taught reading and mathematics to her cousins, Pepe and Ramón. She asked the priest if he would teach those **mysteries** to her, too.

He looked amused. "What does your father say about this?" he asked.

"He says it is not **proper** for women to know all the things men know."

"And what does your mother say?"

"She wanted to know why I need to study books when I will spend my life **keeping house** and raising children."

"And how did you answer her question?"

"I told her the truth. I do not know if it is proper or what I will do with such knowledge. I only know that God has put it into my heart."

"What did she say to that?" asked the priest.

"*Padre*, she said that if God has put it into my heart, then He must have done so for a good reason."

....

mysteries subjects

proper good

keeping house taking care of a house

The priest rubbed his chin and looked at Elena for a long time.

"I think your mother is right. If God wishes you to learn these things, then perhaps you will need them someday. Therefore, I will teach you."

After that, whenever she could get away, Elena walked into the village to study with the priest. Instead of spending her **pesos** on ribbons or **sweets**, she bought books and **tablets**. She kept them under her bed. Elena's mother and her four sisters knew exactly what she was doing, but they pretended they did not. And they kept her secret from Papá.

Elena took to education like a bird to the air. Her mind was soon full of wonderful stories out of the history book—tales of explorers and soldiers and philosophers and kings. Now, when she sat on the veranda with her sewing, great armies marched through her imagination with trumpets blaring and flags flying. As Elena tied

....

pesos money
sweets candy
tablets paper to write on

French knots, Queen Elizabeth was defeating the Spanish **armada**, or Saint Joan was being **burned at the stake**.

Elena loved the numbers, too. Nine was stout and strong. Seven was weak and flabby. Six was jolly, and one was brave. Sometimes they lined up in a row and became large and important. Often they stood on top of one another, and then they either became bigger or smaller. But no matter what they did, there was always only one right answer, and it was Elena's job to find it.

She wondered whether life was like that: a straight road with only one sure **destination**. Then she thought about Columbus and Julius Caesar, and she decided that life was probably many roads, all of them full of surprises.

....

armada warships

burned at the stake killed by fire

destination end

BEFORE YOU MOVE ON...

1. **Conflict** Why didn't Elena's parents want her to learn reading and mathematics?

2. **Paraphrase** Reread pages 11–12. What did Elena mean when she said "God has put it into my heart"?

LOOK AHEAD Read pages 14–16 to find out what else Elena and her father disagree about.

When Elena was sixteen, she met a boy at a *fiesta*. He was neither tall nor especially handsome, but he had large beautiful eyes with which he gazed at her as if she were **the natural wonder of the world**.

"That boy is watching you, Elena," her sisters whispered.

"I know," Elena said.

"He's coming **this way**!" they told her.

"I know," she said again, and she trembled with excitement.

When Pablo came up to them and introduced himself, Elena knew he spoke only to her—though her sister Margarita was much prettier. Elena was glad, too, because she already liked him. He didn't show off as other boys did. There was a peacefulness about him that felt like ancient wisdom. She could tell that he was the sort of person who would **hatch big plans** and work hard to make them come true. She knew

....

the natural wonder of the world the most amazing thing in the world

this way toward us

hatch big plans think of big ideas

he would understand everything she **longed** to tell him. Later, Pablo said that he had seen her standing there in her fiesta dress, listening to the music, and he had known **in a flash** that she was the girl he would marry.

One day Elena went into the parlor where her father was carefully entering figures into his accounts **ledger**. She stood beside him quietly until he looked up. Then she spoke to him of marriage. She told him she **had set her heart on** a boy called Pablo and she would have no one else.

"Nonsense," Elena's father laughed. If she was ready to think about husbands, then he would find her one. He already had his eye on Carlos, the son of a wealthy *hacendado*.

"No, Papá. Carlos is a know-it-all. It is Pablo that I love."

"Pablo is not good enough," he said.

Elena had expected this, for **her sweetheart**

....

longed wanted
in a flash right away; immediately
ledger notebook
had set her heart on wanted to marry
her sweetheart Pablo

was born the son of a poor Tarascan Indian who worked on a big *hacienda*. But both his parents had died, and the hacendado, fond of little Pablo, had taken him into the big house and raised him along with his own children. The boy was dressed in fine clothes, given an education, and taught **the speech and manners of** a gentleman. It was true that he would not inherit lands or money, but Elena didn't care.

She grasped her father's hands and looked at him **beseechingly**. "He is in my heart, Papá," she said. "God put him there, and I cannot get him out."

"Well, you must try. For he is nothing to me, and he can be nothing to you. Wipe your tears and forget him."

....

the speech and manners of how to speak and act like

beseechingly like she was begging

BEFORE YOU MOVE ON...

1. **Cause and Effect** Elena's father did not want her to marry Pablo. Why?

2. **Paraphrase** Reread page 16. What did Papá mean when he said, "For he is nothing to me, and he can be nothing to you"?

LOOK AHEAD Read pages 17–19 to find out if Papá changes his mind.

Rosa continues the story of her mother. Elena starts a new part of her life. There are many changes. Some are wonderful and some are terrible.

Chapter 2

He thought that was the end of it, but it was not. Elena asked herself what Queen Elizabeth would do in her place. What would Saint Joan do? They would be **steadfast and bold**, she decided. Elena would be the same.

When she refused Carlos, Elena's father suggested Roberto, whom she knew to **have a sarcastic wit** and a high opinion of himself.

"No," she said. "No one but Pablo."

"Pablo is not good enough," he said.

If she would not have Roberto, then how about Jorge? Or Raúl?

She refused them all. If she could not marry Pablo, she would grow old in her father's house

---

steadfast and bold sure and strong
have a sarcastic wit tell mean jokes

and never marry at all.

Papá was unmovable, firm as a rock. **It was his habit to be listened to and obeyed.** Yet even rock wears down under the steady work of wind and rain. It loses its roughness. It turns to pebbles, then sand. So Elena **wore her father down at last**, and she married Pablo.

My grandfather had wanted all his daughters to be rich and have important husbands. Yet I think he was secretly glad he lost that battle with Elena. For anyone could see that of all his five girls, none was quite as happy as she was.

Elena and Pablo moved into a little house on the main street. In her sunny *patio* she planted all kinds of flowers and hung little wire cages full of songbirds. As the years passed, the flowers and the birds were joined by babies—first Esteban, then María. I was the third child, and my name is Rosa. The youngest was little Luis.

....

It was his habit to be listened to and obeyed. He expected everyone to listen to him and to do what he said.

wore her father down at last finally got her father to do what she wanted

My father had a shop in the *plaza* where he sold the everyday things that people needed, such as salt, rock sugar, and *manta*, the cotton cloth from which everyone made their clothes.

Then he began to make **fine *sombreros***. He sent to Oaxaca for the gold and silver braid **to trim** the hats. And he brought three Singer sewing machines all the way from Mexico City, carried up the steep mountain slopes on men's backs. The new machines made tiny, perfect stitches. Now my father's sombreros were both sturdy and beautiful. Soon they were famous all over Mexico.

....

fine *sombreros* beautiful hats

to trim to put around the edges of

BEFORE YOU MOVE ON...

1. **Cause and Effect** Papá finally agreed to let Elena marry Pablo. How did this affect Elena?

2. **Narrator** On page 18, a new person starts telling the story. Who is it? How can you tell?

LOOK AHEAD Read pages 20–23 to see what happens to Pablo.

Time passes quickly when you are busy and happy. **It is not human nature to** stop and say, "I must remember this moment, for such a time may not come again." We take happiness for granted. We think there will always be a tomorrow and it will be the same as today. **Great changes take us by surprise.**

In the year 1910, when I was about five years old, my father had to go to Guadalajara on business. He went there once or twice a year. It was nothing unusual. As he **mounted** his horse, my mother went out to say good-bye. "Be careful," she told him. She was worried about who he might meet on the road. We had heard **talk of a revolution**. There were said to be rough soldiers and armed *campesinos* about. They were dangerous men. But Father just squeezed her hand and smiled. "I will be careful," he said.

....

It is not human nature to Most people do not

Great changes take us by surprise. We do not expect big changes to happen.

mounted got on

talk of a revolution that some people wanted to change the government by fighting

Father was joined by several villagers who were making the trip with him. They waved to us and headed off across the rugged countryside, for there were no proper roads. It was just at the end of the rainy season and the path was wet. About an hour after they left, the ground under Father's horse suddenly **gave way, creating a landslide**. Down they plunged into the ravine below.

The villagers raced back for help, and many men hurried off with ropes to haul my father up to safety.

They brought him to our house and laid him on the bed. The doctor came and **dressed** my father's wounds. As he was leaving, we asked the doctor, "Will he live?" He shrugged his shoulders. "Who can tell?" he said. "Perhaps Pablo knows. It is a gift some Indians have."

My mother stood and watched the doctor walk away from our house. "He is right," she

....

gave way, creating a landslide fell away; collapsed and moved down the hill

dressed put medicine and a bandage on

thought to herself. "Pablo knows." So she went into the darkened room and knelt down beside the bed. She took his big hand and gently stroked it.

"Husband," she whispered, "how is it? Do you think you will recover?"

For a long time he did not look at her and he did not answer. At last he turned his head and spoke. "No," he said. Then in a weak but steady voice he told her what he knew. He **named the very day and hour in which** he would die. He said there would be war and that she and the children must leave their home.

"You will always be in my heart," he said. He never spoke again.

Three days later, at the very hour he had spoken, my father died.

Mother went crazy with grief. She ran weeping into the patio, and with a big stick began to swing wildly, knocking down her beautiful flowers. Then she opened all the

....

named the very day and hour in which told her the time when

cages and let the birds free.

After that, my mother grew quiet. Though she went on caring for us just as before, that *chispa*, the **bright spark** that was always a part of her, went out. Papá's absence filled our house with emptiness. I could not really understand what had happened, because I was so young. It seemed to me that Papá had just gone to where I couldn't see him—perhaps he was in the next room. I kept expecting him to walk in our door one day and make everything good again. But he never came, of course, and in time I understood that he never would.

I remember that it was warm and beautiful at that time, the skies a brilliant cloudless blue, day after day. It was as if nature were mocking us.

....

bright spark happiness

BEFORE YOU MOVE ON...

1. **Cause and Effect** How did Pablo die?
2. **Character** Reread pages 22–23. How did Elena show her sadness?

LOOK AHEAD Read pages 24–28 to find out who comes to town.

One day I was playing upstairs with my brother Luis. I heard **the loud clop-clop of horses** on the stone pavement outside—not one, but many horses. So I ran to the window to see. Looking down, I saw our street **transformed into a river of sombreros**. The revolution had reached our little village—it was the army of Pancho Villa riding by!

With a gasp, Mother pulled me away from the window, for Pancho Villa was **a notorious man**. It was true that he was fighting to help free Mexico from the dictator Porfirio Díaz and that he wanted to give back to the campesinos the land that had been stolen from them. He was, in fact, on his way to becoming a genuine folk hero, the Robin Hood of Mexico. But it was also well known that he had once been a **bandit** and that his men were just as bad as the government soldiers. Neither army respected

....

the loud clop-clop of horses the sound of horses as they walked

transformed into a river of sombreros filled with men wearing sombreros

a notorious man known as a bad man

bandit thief, robber

the law. Wherever they went, they stole from people, killed anyone who challenged them, and left burned villages **in their wake**. What would happen to us?

Mother knelt down and gathered us in her arms. She **understood in a flash** that everything that had happened to her before had been for a reason. The books she had read, the hard numbers she had conquered, the battle she had won over her marriage—all this had made her strong. Now she had no father and no husband to help her. She had, instead, great courage and determination. **Had there not always been wars?** And in every country and every age, brave men and women had faced terrible dangers. She could do it, too—God had put it into her heart. We saw this understanding pass across her face like a ripple of light.

....

in their wake behind them

understood in a flash suddenly realized

Had there not always been wars? There had always been wars, right?

"Children," she said urgently, "we must find Esteban."

She knew that soldiers often took older boys and forced them into the army. My brother was sixteen.

None of us had seen him for hours. We searched the house for him, but he wasn't there. A book lay open on his bed. He had put it down and gone off somewhere. Maybe he was out in the streets among all those men. Maybe they had already taken him. At last María found him—up on the roof watching the soldiers. Boys are so foolish sometimes!

We made a hiding place for him in a kitchen cabinet, behind the big clay pots. Then Mother had another thought. **They were sure to steal** the horses. But maybe if they found the stable empty, they would think the horses had already been **seized**. They would certainly not think to look for them in the kitchen, so she brought the horses in there, too.

....

They were sure to steal The soldiers would definitely take
seized taken

Before my mother could hide anything else, there was a loud knock on the door. We could hear deep voices laughing and talking outside. Mother hesitated a moment, wondering what to do. Then she sent us into the back room. We did as we were told but opened the door a crack so we could see what happened. Mother took a deep breath and opened the door.

There stood four or five soldiers, rough men who smelled of sweat and horses. The man in front was stout and **wore a huge drooping mustache**. *Bandoleras* crossed his chest. We had seen his face before, on a government poster. It was Pancho Villa himself!

"Señora," he said, "is this the house of Pablo, the famous maker of sombreros?" It was the last thing she expected to hear.

"It is," she said, "I am his widow."

"Then please **accept my sincere condolences**," said the leader of the rebel army,

....

wore a huge drooping mustache had a long mustache

accept my sincere condolences know that I am truly sorry to hear of his death

bowing slightly. He paused for a moment and then added almost shyly, "And the hats? The fine hats? Are there no more left?"

My mother actually smiled. "Excuse me a minute," she said. She went to a cupboard in her bedroom and returned with one of Father's beautiful silver-trimmed sombreros. "This is the last one," my mother said.

Pancho Villa was delighted. He put it on right away and actually paid her for it. Not only that, he **posted a guard outside our house**. As long as Villa's army was there, we were not harmed.

....

posted a guard outside our house put a soldier by our house to protect us

BEFORE YOU MOVE ON...

1. **Plot** Why did Pancho Villa order soldiers to guard Elena's house?

2. **Character** Reread page 25. What makes Elena good at solving dangerous problems?

LOOK AHEAD Read pages 29–32 to find out how the family gets to safety.

Elena and her children start a new life in a new place. But Elena never forgets her life in Mexico.

Chapter 3

"Pablo was surely watching over us this day," my mother told us later. "**But it may not always be so.** Before your father died, he told me there would be soldiers. He told me we must leave our home. I wonder how I could have forgotten it."

"You were sad, *Mamacita*," María said.

When the *Villistas* had gone, Mother went to the plaza and opened the shop to the people of the village. She emptied the store of everything, taking down **great bolts of manta** and giving them to people who had nothing. We took only our money, some clothes, and food for the journey. We were leaving behind our aunts and uncles, our little house, the furniture, the

....

But it may not always be so. But things might change.
great bolts of manta big rolls of cloth

pictures, the pots and pans and dishes. We said good-bye to the friends **of a lifetime**.

Everyone urged us not to go. "It is not proper for a woman to travel unprotected like that," they said. "It is not safe."

"The world is changing around us," Mother answered. "We must change, too."

We left the village early in the morning. When we reached the train station, we found that it was **packed with frantic**, pushing people. It seemed as though everyone in Mexico was trying to get on that train. Mother and María managed to make it inside. Then before Esteban got on, he handed Luis and me in through the window, along with the basket of food.

We were lucky to have benches to sit on. Most of the people were in **boxcars** or crowded in the aisles.

For five days the train chugged north.

---

of a lifetime we had known all our lives
packed with frantic filled with frightened
boxcars train cars that were for supplies

Through the open windows came soot, dust, and flies. I had worn a beautiful lacy white dress for the trip. Soon it was damp with sweat and covered with dirt.

When we reached Ciudad Juárez, we faced a new problem. What were we to do with Esteban? He was tall, almost a man. The soldiers at the border crossing would not treat him as a child. They might detain him for days, together with the rough men from the train. They might take him for the army.

"I think the answer will come to me," Mother told us. "We must be patient."

So we waited while she thought, but it was not a good place to be. The town was rough and **lawless**. With thousands of refugees pouring in, desperate to **flee** homes that were no longer safe, thieves and **pickpockets** roamed the streets. Hotels and shops charged ridiculous prices that people had to pay, because they had

....

lawless people did not obey the laws
flee leave
pickpockets robbers

no other choice but to starve or sleep in the streets. For days we ate nothing but fruit.

Mother **befriended** a Chinese fruit seller who was honest and kind. One day she told him our problem. He smiled, for he knew exactly how to help us. Every day he crossed the border with his fruit wagon. We could dress Esteban in the man's clothes and straw hat. He would pretend to be the fruit seller's helper.

That afternoon we went over the bridge to El Paso together, Mother and the three of us walking along next to the fruit wagon. The cost was one penny each. At last we were safely in the United States.

....

befriended became friends with

BEFORE YOU MOVE ON...

1. **Character's Motive** Why did Elena leave her home even though everyone told her not to?
2. **Plot** Reread pages 31–32. Why did Esteban cross the border with the fruit seller?

LOOK AHEAD Read pages 33–37 to find out what life in the United States is like.

We headed for California because we had a cousin, Trinidad, who lived there. We didn't have his address, though. In fact, we didn't even know what town he lived in. So we went to San Francisco, which was famous. We made our way to the *barrio*, where many people from Mexico lived. We asked everyone we met there, "Do you know our cousin Trinidad?" No one did. And besides, we didn't like it there. It was damp and cold. In Los Angeles, no one **had heard of** Trinidad, either. We were happier there, because the weather was warmer. But the city was too big, not like our lovely little village in Mexico. We heard about a place called Santa Ana. There were lemon and orange and walnut **groves** there and good schools for the children. So that is where we went and that is where we stayed. We never did find Trinidad.

By then, we had spent most of our money. So Esteban got a job picking fruit. Sometimes he was gone for weeks, living in the camps near the farms. When he came home he was sore

....

had heard of knew about
groves trees

and tired. He didn't laugh and play with me the way he had before.

Mother **ran a boardinghouse**, which was hard work. She did the cleaning, made the beds, mopped the floors, and scrubbed the bathtub. She washed and ironed the boarders' clothes. After all that, she went into the kitchen and cooked **mountains of** rice and beans and *tortillas* and *enchiladas* for them to eat. We all sat down to dinner together at a long pine table. Sometimes the boarders were very nice and became our friends. Some even came from the same part of Mexico as our family had. It made me feel like I wasn't so far from home.

María and I did what we could. We hung the laundry out on the clothesline, and we brought it back in if it rained. We helped wash the dishes and changed all the sheets once a week. And we looked after little Luis.

But Mother said that our real job was to get an education. School and homework always came first. When we were done with that, she

----

ran a boardinghouse rented out rooms in a house
mountains of huge amounts of

said, we could help. I felt bad sometimes, sitting in a chair with a book in my lap while Mother **was never still, always bustling about** at her chores. She did it **with a good spirit**, though. If I said to her, "You work too hard, Mamacita," she would just shake her head and smile.

"And what is so bad about work?" she would say. "Work is how I take care of my family. Work is how I keep busy. Work is how I am useful. It is not so bad."

At school we learned to speak English and heard all about George Washington crossing the Delaware and Thomas Jefferson writing the Declaration of Independence. We wrote essays on the American Revolution and the American Civil War, and one day **it dawned on me** that Americans had suffered in terrible wars just as we had. And not long after that, I realized that Americans weren't "they" anymore. After all, we wore American clothes, read American

....

was never still, always bustling about worked all the time
with a good spirit happily
it dawned on me I realized

books, knew American songs, and ate American candy. We had all become *real* Americans—all of us, that is, but Mamá.

She never quite knew what she was. Part of her was still back in Mexico and part of her was with us in California. Sometimes in the evening, after the dishes were done, we all went out on the porch to sit and enjoy the cool night air. At those times, Mother liked to talk about the **old days**. She told us about growing up in her father's great house in the beautiful mountains of Mexico. She talked of her gentle sisters who sang so beautifully to the guitar. She remembered her own little house full of flowers and birds. But she especially loved to talk about Father—how they fell in love first and got to know each other later, how he was such an artist, making beautiful sombreros, and how he knew things it was impossible to know, yet he knew them just the same. I had been so small when Father died, I could

....

She never quite knew what she was. She never knew whether she was Mexican or American.

old days past

scarcely remember him. Those stories **gave him back to me**.

In all those years she talked only of happy times. It was much later that we learned what had happened in our little village. Only when we were grown—strong and full of hope—did we find out that it was gone, burned to the ground by the soldiers. And when we heard about the people who had died, people we had known, then we understood what our mother had done. With her courage and **daring**, she had saved us all.

....

gave him back to me helped me remember him

daring brave actions

BEFORE YOU MOVE ON...

1. **Comparisons** How was the family's life in the United States different from their life in Mexico?

2. **Summarize** Reread page 35. How did Elena feel about work?

LOOK AHEAD Read pages 38–40 to find out how Elena helps her daughter Rosa.

Sometimes while I was growing up, I would come to Mamá with a problem that seemed **deep and terrible** to me. Maybe some girl had said something mean about the way I looked or hadn't invited me to her party. Or I was miserable because I could not understand **positive and negative numbers**. Or had made a bad grade. Or liked a boy who didn't like me. "Yes, I understand," Mamá would say, stroking my hair. "But, *chiquita*, this is not a big thing. It will be over and then it will soon be forgotten. You are much bigger than this problem."

I would deny it with all my heart. **Who was I to withstand the disaster of the moment?** It was big, so very, very big! That was always when she would tell her stories again. She would talk about how much she had wanted an education, even though it wasn't what girls were supposed to do and her parents didn't approve.

....

deep and terrible really hard; really big

positive and negative numbers something hard in mathematics

Who was I to withstand the disaster of the moment? How could I survive the problem I was having?

Yet she had achieved it! How she had wanted to marry Pablo because she knew he was a good man, though he had no money and her father **forbade it**. But she had married him all the same, hadn't she? Then she had lost Papá, and she didn't believe she could be strong anymore. And yet she was. And when war came, she had to leave everything she had ever known and go off to a strange new country so that her children could grow up safe. Now that was a big thing! But she had been bigger even than a war—and here we all were in California!

My mother said that she had always known where to look when she was frightened or confused. Something powerful inside **her very being** told her who she was and what was worth fighting for. Mamá said that same thing is in all of us—we have only to look deep inside ourselves. The answers are always there, she

....

forbade it would not let her marry him
her very being her soul; her spirit

said, and the courage, too. God has written them in our hearts.

BEFORE YOU MOVE ON...

1. **Generalization** What did Rosa learn from Mamá about solving problems?

2. **Paraphrase** Reread page 39. What did Rosa mean when she said Mamá had been bigger even than a war?

LOOK AHEAD Read pages 41–44 to learn more about the Mexican Revolution.

The author tells the history of the Mexican Revolution. Between 1910 and 1920, many people left Mexico because of the war. Like Elena's family, they moved to the United States.

Historical Note

The Mexican Revolution of 1910 to 1920 is unfamiliar to many Americans. Yet it was **the most significant social movement in the New World during our century** and the first of three great revolutions in a decade, followed first by Russia, then China. As many as a million people may have died before the Mexican war was over.

For more than thirty years, Mexico had been ruled by a dictator, Porfirio Díaz. Though his government had brought stability and wealth

....

the most significant social movement in the New World during our century the most important thing to happen in North and South America between 1900 and 2000

to the country, **the vast majority** of the people could not enjoy it. The gap between the rich *hacendados*, who owned great estates, or *haciendas*, and the poor *campesinos*, had always been great. But Díaz **so favored the rich** that he took the village farmlands, the *ejidos*, away from the people who depended on them to grow food and sold them to the hacendados. By 1910, fewer than a thousand families controlled the land of Mexico, and around ten million Mexican Indians had become landless **serfs**.

So great was the misery of the Mexican people that they rose up, under the leadership of Francisco Madero, **to drive Díaz out of office**. To face the government soldiers, or *federales*, Madero gathered an army of campesinos, led by brave and passionate men who **were fired by a common cause**. The

....

the vast majority almost all

so favored the rich liked the rich people so much better than the poor people

serfs peasants, field workers

to drive Díaz out of office to make Díaz leave the government

were fired by a common cause believed in the same thing

most famous of these rebel generals were Emiliano Zapata, who fought mostly in the south of Mexico, and the notorious ex-bandit Pancho Villa, with his fearsome División del Norte. By May 1911, the rebels drove Porfirio Díaz out of office, and by November, Madero became president of Mexico.

But the war was **far from over**. Madero governed only fifteen months before a counterrevolution forced him to resign. Three days later, he was assassinated. The bloody civil war raged on in Mexico for eight more years. **Three consecutive presidents** played their brief parts in the spectacle of national revolution before **peace was finally restored**.

Over the ten years that Mexico was locked in civil war, wave after wave of refugees fled the country, most of them heading north to the United States via El Paso, Texas, as Elena's family did. Today, many Americans

....

far from over not over at all

Three consecutive presidents Three presidents, one after the other,

peace was finally restored Mexico had peace again

can trace their roots to grandparents or great-grandparents who came here during the Mexican Revolution, as so many others had before them, seeking safety in dangerous times.

....

can trace their roots to can name

BEFORE YOU MOVE ON...

1. **Summarize** What started the Mexican Revolution?

2. **Inference** Reread pages 43 and 44. Then look at the map on page 4. Why do you think so many Mexicans traveled to the United States?

Glossary

bandolera—a belt worn over the shoulders and across the chest, used to hold bullets

barrio—a neighborhood in the United States, usually of Spanish-speaking people

campesino—a rural worker

chiquita—a young girl

chispa—a spark or sparkle

ejido—land held by a community

enchilada—a tortilla served with chili

federales—soldiers in the Mexican army

fiesta—a festival or holiday

hacendado—the owner of a hacienda

hacienda—a large estate or plantation

mamacita—an endearment for mother

manta—a rough cotton cloth

padre—father; a Catholic priest

patio—an open courtyard, usually at the center of a house

plaza—a public square or marketplace

siesta—a nap, often taken at the hottest part of the day

sombrero—a wide-brimmed hat, often made of straw

tortilla—a thin corn or wheat bread, eaten with most Mexican meals

veranda—a porch on the outside of a house

Villista—a soldier in Pancho Villa's army